The Birth of Jesus

D0468261

by
B. A. Ramsbottom

GOSPEL STANDARD TRUST
PUBLICATIONS
1992
12b Roundwood Lane, Harpenden,
Herts. AL5 3DD, England.

Bethlehem

A poor man and his wife were going on a long, tiring journey. How they were travelling we do not know – whether walking, or perhaps on a donkey. They were on their way to a little town called Bethlehem. The man's name was Joseph and his wife was called Mary.

They must have been very weary when they arrived as they had come a long way. But there was nowhere they could stay. The inn where most people stayed was full. There was no room at all for them. What a disappointment! What could they do? Stay out all night in the streets?

The best place they could find was a stable – a place where cows or horses are kept. It would be cold and not too clean. Not a very nice place! But it was better than sleeping outside.

And that very night Mary had a baby boy. His name was Jesus. And when He had been wrapped up, the only place there was to put Him was in the manger – the trough in which the cows fed. We wonder if there were any cows with their little calves there at the time? Or horses or donkeys stabled there?

Why was the baby called Jesus? (It means "the Saviour.") Well, long before that night an angel from heaven had come to visit Mary and had told her she was going to have a baby, and God Himself would be that baby's Father – not Joseph. The baby was to be different from all other babies because He was the Son of God.

Then, later, the angel had come to Joseph and told him too about this wonderful baby. He had told Joseph what His name would be. He was to be called Jesus "for He shall save His people from their sins."

So now this wonderful baby had been born – in a stable. How Joseph and Mary loved that little baby as He lay there in the manger! And God in heaven was pleased.

Yet all Bethlehem was asleep. And no one knew what a wonderful thing had taken place.

God had said that when He sent His Son He would be born in the little town of Bethlehem. That is why, just before the baby's birth, Joseph and Mary had to leave their home in Nazareth. The Roman rulers had commanded them to go to Bethlehem so their names could be written down for taxing.

Perhaps some of you have a baby brother or sister. How carefully everything was made ready before they were born; but when Jesus, the Son of God came, He was born in a poor stable. How great His love!

There is a verse which says: "Ye know the grace

of our Lord Jesus Christ, that though He was rich, yet for your sakes He became poor."

You can read this story in Luke chapter 2, verses 1 to 7. See also Matthew chapter 1, verses 18 to 25, and Luke chapter 1, verses 26 to 37.

O little town of Bethlehem,
    How still we see thee lie;
Above thy deep and dreamless sleep
    The silent stars go by;
Yet in thy dark streets shineth
    The everlasting light;
The hopes and fears of all the years
    Are met in thee tonight.

"This is a faithful saying, and worthy of all acceptation, that Christ Jesus came into the world to save sinners; of whom I am chief" (1 Timothy 1. 15).

The Shepherds

Out in the fields outside Bethlehem there were shepherds looking after their sheep. Though it was the middle of the night they still had to be there. Perhaps a lion or bear was prowling about, waiting to seize a little lamb. Each night, whether cold or hot, wet or dry, there they had to be watching their sheep out in the fields.

But whatever is happening? Who is that bright figure they can see? And what is that dazzling light that is shining round about them? They were terrified. Surely this must be an angel!

But then the angel spoke to them – so kindly. He told them there was no need for them to be frightened. He had come from heaven to tell them about the wonderful baby who had been born in Bethlehem while everyone was asleep. This baby was "the Saviour, Christ the Lord."

The shepherds were amazed to hear that the long expected Saviour had now come. But what a shock! If they wanted to find the baby, they would not have to go to a palace, certainly not to King Herod's palace. They would find the baby, of all places, "lying in a manger." So first they must look for a stable!

But before they had time to do anything, or even talk to one another, suddenly the sky was filled

with a host of glorious angels, all singing:

"GLORY TO GOD IN THE HIGHEST, AND ON EARTH PEACE, GOOD WILL TOWARD MEN."

It must have been the sweetest song that was ever heard on earth. But think of it! The wonderful baby is born in Bethlehem. The Saviour has come, but no one knows, no one cares. Yet God sends a host of holy angels, bright and glorious, from heaven to celebrate the birth of His beloved Son. Jesus always had been the Son of God; but now He had come to earth to be born as a baby.

Then the angels disappeared. They had gone back to heaven. The shepherds looked at one another. "Let us go to Bethlehem, and see this thing," they said. They knew that it was God who had let them know. How kind and gracious of the great God in heaven to send a message about Jesus to a few poor shepherds!

So they hurried as quickly as they could to find the stable and the manger. But what about the sheep? Well, they could trust God to look after them. Really, now they had heard such good news, they must forget about everything else.

And there, when they had reached the town, they found everything just as God had said – "Mary, and Joseph, and the babe lying in a manger."

What do you think they did? They were so pleased that they told everyone what had happened, and everyone was amazed. But we do not read of one single person going to find the Saviour. How strange!

We do not know what happened afterwards to the shepherds. We do not even know their names, or how many there were, or whether they were old or young. But the last we hear of them is that they were praising God. Their hearts were full of joy. They had seen the long-expected Saviour, Jesus the Son of God.

You can read this story in Luke chapter 2, verses 8 to 19.

Angels from the realms of glory,
　　Wing your flight o'er all the earth;
Ye who sang creation's story,
　　Now proclaim Messiah's birth;
　　　Come and worship,
Worship Christ, the new-born King.

"He was in the world, and the world was made by Him, and the world knew Him not. He came unto His own, and His own received Him not. But as many as received Him, to them gave He power to become the sons of God, even to them that believe on His name" (John 1. 10-13).

Mary

When the shepherds had left the stable, Jesus' mother Mary did not say anything. She was silent. Often we read of Mary being silent. But there were many things she was thinking about.

Did she think about what the angel told her before Jesus was born? "He shall be great, and shall be called the Son of the highest." And did she think about the beautiful hymn she composed? (Did you know that Mary wrote a lovely hymn?) It begins, "My soul doth magnify the Lord, and my spirit hath rejoiced in God my Saviour."

At this time though, she must have wondered especially at the story the shepherds had told her – of the angel, and what he had said, and the host of angels from heaven and their song.

Yes, Mary, was a very happy woman. She had the great blessing of having a baby different from all other babies that have ever been born. She knew that this baby was truly God. How she loved Him and cared for Him! And we know that as Jesus grew up, He dearly loved His mother, and was always kind to her.

Some people worship Mary but we must not do this; we must only worship God. Nor can we pray to Mary for Mary is now dead.

How amazing that Mary's baby is true, almighty

God!

> No less almighty at His birth,
> Than on His throne supreme;
> His shoulders held up heaven and earth,
> When Mary held up Him.

You can read about Mary especially in Luke chapter 1, verses 26 to 56, and Luke chapter 2, verses 16 to 19 (as well as the passages given in the other chapters).

> He dwelt in the manger,
> That heavenly Stranger,
> Where oxen had trod;
> And she who found favour
> With God called Him Saviour,
> And knew Him as God.

"When the fulness of the time was come, God sent forth His Son, made of a woman, made under the law, to redeem them that were under the law" (Galatians 4. 4, 5).

> Once in royal David's city,
> Stood a lowly cattle shed,
> Where a mother laid her baby
> In a manger for His bed:
> Mary was that mother mild,
> Jesus Christ her little child.

Simeon

At this time there was an old man who lived in Jerusalem, about six miles away from Bethlehem. He was a good and gracious man, and he had a secret. God had told him that before he died he would actually see the long-expected Saviour, the Lord Jesus Christ. Many good people had hoped that one day they would see Him, but they had been disappointed.

One day something special seemed to be happening. Simeon felt that he must go along to the temple. He had been there many times in his life, but now God was speaking to him telling him he *must* go today. So along he went.

And then something happened. A man and his wife entered the temple. Nothing strange about that. But it was Joseph and Mary and they were carrying the baby Jesus. He was now just over a month old. They were doing what God had told them to do – presenting the baby to God in the temple, and offering a sacrifice. And the only sacrifice they could afford was the one poor people offered: not a lamb, or a bull, but just two pigeons.

As Simeon looked on the pair, he realised that this little baby was his Saviour and his God. The long-awaited day had come. O how happy he must have been! God had done what He promised, and

there was his Lord before his eyes.

Like some old prophet Simeon picked up the Lord Jesus and held Him in his arms. Then he thanked God for all His kindness and love. He felt willing to die. He had got what he had been waiting for. He said, "Lord, now lettest Thou Thy servant depart in peace, according to Thy Word: for mine eyes have seen Thy salvation."

Those who wait for God are not disappointed.

Joseph and Mary listened intently. How amazed they were to hear some of the wonderful things Simeon said about the baby!

Simeon ended by blessing them. But then he had some sad things to say. He told Mary of the sorrow which she would one day know.

So while He was still a baby there was this reminder that "Christ was born to die." He had been born at Bethlehem, but one day He must suffer and die on the cross at Calvary.

You can read this story in Luke chapter 2, verses 25 to 35.

He came down to earth from heaven
  Who is God and Lord of all;
And His shelter was a stable,
  And His cradle was a stall;
  With the poor, and mean, and lowly,
  Lived on earth our Saviour holy.

"For unto us a child is born, unto us a son is given: and the government shall be upon His shoulder: and His name shall be called Wonderful, Counseller, The mighty God, The everlasting Father, The Prince of Peace" (Isaiah 9. 6).

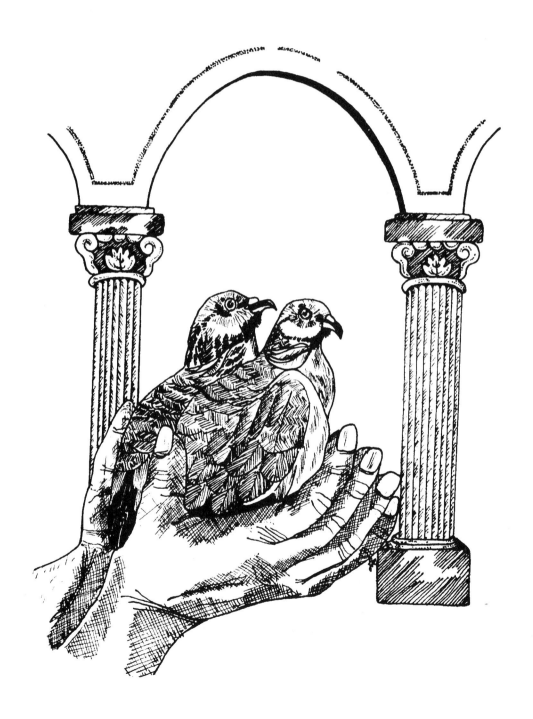

Anna

Every day in this temple at Jerusalem a very aged woman could be seen. She was there all the time. Her name was Anna.

Many years ago, when Anna was young, something very sad had happened to her. She had been married – but not long after her husband had died. A bitter sorrow!

But Anna was a gracious woman, and all her life had been spent in serving God. Day and night alike she could be found praying to Him. I wonder how often we pray?

Now Anna was a prophetess, and so she knew all about God's promises and what He had said He would do. She knew that one day His own Son would be born as a baby in Bethlehem. Like Simeon she was one of those who were longing for His coming.

At the exact moment when Simeon was holding the Lord Jesus in his arms, who should come along but Anna? God saw that she was there "in that instant." And she too was so delighted. She poured out her heart in thanks to God for the wonderful gift of His own Son.

Now, as well as Simeon and Anna, there were a few others in Jerusalem who were waiting for the coming of Jesus and longing for Him to come. We are told they "looked for redemption." They knew that when Jesus came He would redeem His people with His own blood.

And God saw that all these knew what had happened, that the Son of God had come. An angel told the shepherds. A star told the wise men. God Himself told Simeon. But it was Anna that God sent to tell the wonderful news to these different ones in Jerusalem.

We can think of this aged woman slowly walking from house to house, so happy to tell them that the Lord had come. And how happy they must have been to hear the joyful tidings!

You can read this story in Luke chapter 2, verses 36 to 38.

> Hail, thou ever-blessed morn!
> Hail, redemption's happy dawn!
> Sing through all Jerusalem:
> Christ is born in Bethlehem!

"For unto you is born this day in the city of David a Saviour, which is Christ the Lord" (Luke 2. 11).

The Wise Men

Far away in an eastern land lived some wise men. We wonder why they were called wise men? It seems that they were very clever and studied all kinds of things. They must also have been rich. Perhaps they were kings. (Many people have thought so.)

How many wise men there were we are not told. People usually talk about "the three wise men." Well, perhaps there were three – but the Bible does not tell us.

One night these wise men were looking up into the sky. But what was this they could see, something that they had never seen before? A bright shining star. Often the eastern sky was full of stars – but this one? No, they had never seen it before. It was different.

And God showed them why the star was there. A wonderful King had been born and if they followed the star, it would lead them to where He could be found.

How pleased they were that God had told them about the new-born King! They must go at once to find Him. But wait! First of all, they must find some lovely presents to take for Him. If you ever go to visit a new baby, you always take a present, don't you? So when they had got the presents, they

left everything and off they set.

It must have been a long, long journey – many, many miles. But on they went, following the star. If they felt lonely or sad, or wondered if they should go back home, there was the star still going on before them. Whatever else, they wanted to find the new-born King.

At last they reached the holy city of Jerusalem. Eagerly they looked forward to seeing the baby King so they hastened to the palace, expecting He would be there.

But something is wrong! What is the matter? No one seems to know anything about any baby King. There is no baby in the palace. King Herod does not know what they are talking about. And he does not seem very pleased!

How disappointing! Had they made a bad mistake? Had they just been imagining things?

No! Those who truly seek for Jesus will always find Him at last.

You can read this story in Matthew chapter 2, verses 1 to 7.

As with gladness men of old
Did the guiding star behold,
As with joy they hailed its light,
Leading onwards, beaming bright,
So, most gracious Lord, may we
Evermore be led to Thee.

"The Lord shall arise upon thee, and His glory shall be seen upon thee. And the Gentiles shall come to Thy light, and kings to the brightness of Thy rising" (Isaiah 60. 2, 3).

Herod

Herod the king was very troubled. He was a wicked man, cruel and unkind. What was this he had just heard? A baby born who was to be King? But who was the baby? Herod had heard nothing. Was this baby going to grow up and throw Herod off his throne?

Something must be done. And quickly!

Herod began to think of what he had often heard. A glorious Person would one day come who would be King of the Jews. For years and years people had spoken of the coming of this great King – Christ (or Messiah) as He was known.

And then Herod had a wicked thought. If he could find this baby, then he would have Him killed. Cruel Herod! But where could He have been born? Did anyone know?

So Herod gathered together all those who knew the Scriptures well. He had a question to ask them. Do they tell us where Christ will be born?

Really, it was an easy question. There was no problem. They could tell Herod straight away. "Yes," they said, "in Bethlehem." Not very far away – only about six miles.

The Scriptures were so plain. Many years ago a prophet called Micah had foretold that it would be Bethlehem where Christ should be born.

So Herod sent for the wise men. Everyone else had to go out, and then he very carefully asked them: how long ago was it since they first saw this star? Then he told them to go to Bethlehem.

"Keep on searching till you find this child," he said. "Don't forget to come back and tell me where He is." And then Herod told a terrible lie. He said, "I want to come and worship Him." You all know what Herod really wanted to do, don't you? Yes, kill Jesus.

So once again the wise men set out on their travels. And they were so happy when they saw the star again.

But the star would not have led them to the wrong place. The star had not taken them to Herod's palace. They must have thought when they got to Jerusalem it was all easy now; they didn't need the star. What a mistake! They were so glad to see the star once more.

And the star went before them till it "stood over where the young child was."

Some children think of the shepherds and the wise men coming together to visit Jesus. No. The shepherds came the night He was born; the wise men a long time after. How long we do not know, but Joseph and Mary and Jesus were now in a house in Bethlehem, not the stable.

You can read this story in Matthew chapter 2, verses 1 to 10.

The star drew nigh to the north-west,
O'er Bethlehem it took its rest,
And there it did both stop and stay,
Right over the place where Jesus lay.

"But thou, Bethlehem Ephratah, though thou be little among the thousands of Judah, yet out of thee shall He come forth unto Me that is to be ruler in Israel; whose goings forth have been from of old, from everlasting" (Micah 5. 2).

The Wise Men Worship Jesus

What is this noise outside the little house in Bethlehem? And who are these strangers waiting to come in? It was the wise men, and they entered the house.

Joseph and Mary were not used to visitors like this – rich, and they had come so far.

We wonder if the wise men were shocked? or disappointed? or sad? They had come all this way to find a new-born King – and at long last the star had led them, not to a palace, or a rich man's dwelling, but to this humble house, the home of a poor man and a poor woman (not a king and queen).

But how wonderful! As soon as "they saw the young child, they fell down and worshipped Him." You think of it! These wise men, falling down before the little Lord Jesus, and worshipping Him as God. They were *not* disappointed. They had found what they wanted. They were satisfied.

May we too be taught to seek for the Lord Jesus and not be satisfied till we find Him.

But now what is happening? The wise men are producing expensive gifts and presenting them to the Lord Jesus.

First of all there is precious gold – a very suitable present for a king.

Next, there is sweet smelling frankincense – a kind of perfume used in the temple for worshipping God. And so fitting because Jesus is God.

But the third present is very strange. Myrrh! Why myrrh? Myrrh was not for a little child; myrrh was used when someone was dead. Ah! it was a reminder that Jesus had come that one day He might die on the cross, die to save His people from their sins.

Then, having given these beautiful, expensive presents, the wise men left. Joseph and Mary must have been amazed.

But did the wise men go back and tell Herod what they had found? No. That night when the wise men fell asleep they had a strange dream. God spoke to them. He told them *not* to go and tell Herod, but to go straight back to their own land.

We love to think of the wise men and their visit. And we wonder what they had to say to each other as they journeyed back to their home in the east?

Herod the king was angry. He was furious. He felt the wise men were laughing at him. Why had they not come back to him? Why had they not done what he said? Why did they not believe him?

Then Herod did something terrible. He sent men out to find all the tiny children who were not more than two years old, and cruelly kill them. It is no wonder that we always think of Herod as a terribly wicked man. He was determined no one else was going to be king in his place.

But what of the little Lord Jesus? Was He not killed too?

You can read this story in Matthew chapter 2, verses 11 to 16.

Born a King on Bethlehem's plain,
    Gold I bring to crown Him again,
King for ever, ceasing never
    Over His saints to reign.

Frankincense to offer have I,
    Incense owns a Deity nigh;
Prayer and praising, voices raising,
    Worship Him, God most high.

Myrrh is mine; its bitter perfume
    Breathes a life of gathering gloom:
Sorrowing, sighing, bleeding, dying,
    Sealed in the stone-cold tomb.

"O worship the Lord in the beauty of holiness" (Psalm 96. 9).

The Flight into Egypt

It is night. Everything is dark. Who are these figures that can hardly be seen stealing out of Bethlehem? A man, a woman, and a child. Yes, Joseph, Mary and the little child Jesus. They are escaping from Herod's cruel plan to kill all the little children around Bethlehem.

A long journey is before them. They are on their way to Egypt, where once the baby Moses floated in his ark of bulrushes on the River Nile. The Lord Jesus was to be safe from danger there. Herod's plan had failed.

But why Egypt? Like the wise men, Joseph too had had a strange dream, and he too had been told what a cruel thing Herod was going to do. God in heaven was lovingly watching over His beloved Son and taking care of Him. So He told Joseph to flee with Mary and Jesus down into the land of Egypt.

We are interested to know what happened while Joseph and Mary and Jesus lived in Egypt. It must have been strange for them, away from God's people. We wonder who they met and what they saw – perhaps the pyramids.

But at last wicked Herod died, and Joseph had another remarkable dream. This time it was an angel telling him that Herod was no longer alive.

They can all go back now into the land of Israel.

Joseph and Mary must have been glad, mustn't they? It was a long, long time since the two of them had left Nazareth on their journey to Bethlehem. And many, many wonderful things had happened since. How much they had to talk about!

At last there they were, back in their own Nazareth once more. And so this holy child, the Lord Jesus, in His wonderful life, became known as "Jesus of Nazareth."

How great the love of the Lord Jesus in coming into this sinful world to be born – and to die!

You can read this story in Matthew chapter 2, verses 13 to 15 and 19 to 23.

Jesus who lived above the sky,
Came down to be a Man and die;
And in the Bible we may see,
How very good He used to be.

But such a cruel death He died,
He was hung up and crucified;
And those kind hands that did such good,
They nailed them to a cross of wood.

And so He died, and this is why
He came to be a Man and die:
The Bible says He came from heaven,
That souls might have their sins forgiven.

He knew how wicked men had been,
And knew that God must punish sin,
So for His people Jesus said,
He'd bear the punishment instead.

"Greater love hath no man than this, that a man lay down His life for His friends" (John 15. 13).

"Herein is love, not that we loved God, but that He loved us, and sent His Son to be the propitiation for our sins" (1 John 4. 10).